Why Do We Need This Book?

CW01604126

After a death children may feel ignored. The parents may be too distressed to notice the child's needs. The child may try to protect them from more distress by concealing their own needs.

This handbook provides the knowledge and tools to enable any healthcare professional to help a bereaved child. By providing support you could prevent years of problems or even a suicide.

This is a handbook not a text book. A few references are provided plus a reading list for those interested in further study. The guidance provided here is a mixture of current best practice, research evidence and years of experience.

Throughout the book we discuss the role of parents. For "parents" please read "parent(s) or carers". If you use this book, please let us know how it can be improved for the next edition, using the form at the back.

PENHALIGON'S FRIENDS

First published in Great Britain in 2006 by
Penhaligon's Friends PO Box 11 Camborne Cornwall TR14 8YG

© Compiled by Dr Simon Barton MB BS, MRCGP, DRCOG, DCH, Doreen Hocking BSN & Wendy Ball RN, PCET
© Illustrations & Design by Jenny Nightingale www.jennynightingale.co.uk

Sponsored by THE DUCHY Health CHARITY

ISBN 0-9550757-1-8

Foreword

Most children see, hear and understand more than adults realise. They know when those around them are worried. When someone they love dies, or when they lose a pet, they grieve, sometimes silently, and they suffer. This suffering may go unnoticed because as a society we do not like to dwell on death or talk about bereavement openly. Moreover for many children, the death of a close relative is thankfully not common unlike the experience of their grandparents or great-grandparents in childhood. This means that, when it happens, the support systems in the family to deal with grief are not developed.

I am a retired paediatrician. Over the years I saw many children with so-called psychosomatic illnesses such as tummy-aches, headaches or pains in the arms and legs. Most of these children had real pain, sufficient to interfere with their lives and to keep them away from school. By far the commonest cause was some form of psychological stress and by far the commonest psychological stress was some unresolved grief or fear of death. Very young children readily accept imaginary concepts such as the existence of Father Christmas, and notions such as heaven and an afterlife are equally accepted by them. Around the age of eight years they become aware of a different reality and fear of separation from those that they love can become all too real, albeit hidden and unspoken. Encouraging them to talk about these feelings is important. When physical symptoms become the manifestation of this stress, then recognition of the cause and sympathetic support whilst encouraging the child to talk about their fear is often sufficient to achieve a cure.

This book is important. It needs to be read by all professionals who deal with children; doctors, nurses, schoolteachers, counsellors, therapists and most particularly by parents. I commend and thank Dr Simon Barton and his colleagues in Penhaligon's Friends for writing it. I am sure it already has been, and will continue to be, of inestimable benefit to children generally and especially to those who have suffered the terrible trauma of losing someone they love.

Sir Cyril Chantler

Chairman, Great Ormond Street Hospital for Sick Children and the King's Fund, London.

Contents

Remember Me Too

How Children Grieve

The way children experience and react to death may be different from an adult. One of the differences is that intense emotion and behavioural expression are not continuous in children. A child's grief may appear to be more intermittent and brief than an adult's but in fact usually lasts longer. (Worden J 1996). Adults could be said to wade through rivers of grief; for children their grief is more like jumping in and out of puddles. One minute a child may be crying and upset, the next laughing and playing; this is normal.

Children's Response to Grief

The way a child responds to grief is influenced by many factors such as: the type of death, the relationship, the grieving process of their carer and the age of the child. There is a wide variation in how children grieve when someone has died.

The reactions can be:

* Shock and disbelief
* Dismay and protest
* Apathy and being stunned
* Continuation of normal activities

(Dyregrov, A. 1990)

A child's concept of death and dying changes as his or her understanding develops with increasing age. Broadly speaking, it follows these patterns:

Infants

* No understanding of death
* Absorb emotion of those around them

Age 2-3 Years

* Often confuse death with sleep
* May exhibit loss of speech (Wass H. Corr C 1984)

Age 3- 6 years

* This is the age of magical thinking. Children may believe their actions and words caused the death or that they can bring the dead person back.
* Do not always have the words to express feelings
* May exhibit disturbances in eating, sleeping and bladder control (Grollman.E.A 1990)

Age 6-9 years

* Beginning to understand the finality of death
* Afraid that death is contagious and worry about who else is going to die
* May ask questions over and over again
* Often protect adults
* Usually very curious about death
* May have a strong sense of abandonment (Wass H. Corr C 1984)

9-12 years

* View death as inevitable
* Understanding is nearer to adults
* Beginning to understand the finality of death
* Aware of the impact the death will have on them

13-18 years

* Understand the finality and universality of death (Grollman.E.A 1990)
* More interested in talking to peers than to their family
* Often participate in risk-taking behaviour

Tasks of Grief

William Worden (1991) suggests that grief is an essential and painful healing process, which is achieved through a series of tasks:

* Facing reality
* Experiencing the pain of grief
* Adjusting to the new reality
* Re-investing in the future and moving on with life

Some children may not be able to acknowledge what has happened and may cope by denying it at first. It may help a child face the reality if he is given the opportunity to see the dead person and to be involved in the preparations for the funeral preparations and their attendance at the funeral will help them.

Serious Illness

Serious illness within the family can disrupt family life causing emotional, social and financial difficulties.

When Someone is Seriously Ill Children Need:

* To be given information a bit at a time
* To have information repeated in words they can understand
* To be involved in the care of the ill person (if they would like to)
* To hear words such as cancer and death used when appropriate

(Adults need to check that the child understands these words)

Avoid euphemisms such as "big C" for cancer

* To be allowed to ask questions and have them answered honestly
* To be told what is going to happen
* To be told how it may affect them
* To know who will be around to help them
* To express feelings, in words, play & art
* To be given an opportunity to express their anxieties and to receive reassurance where appropriate.
* To spend quality time with their family
* To be allowed to say good-bye.
* To play and have fun
* To have a routine

"The most meaningful help that we can give any child is to share his feelings before the event of the death and allow him to work through the feelings, whether they are rational or irrational".
(Kubler Ross 1983)

Remember

Don't be afraid to say "I don't know"

Try not to make promises that you may be unable to keep.

Share your own feelings openly with the child

The school or early years setting should be informed so they can support the child too.

How Children Might React to the Illness of Someone Close to them

Children's experience of and reaction to serious illness may be different from that of adults. Reactions will vary according to age, personality and previous experience. These can include:

* Being overwhelmed
* Seeming not to care as they try to hide their emotions
* Appearing to cope well and accepting the situation

6 year old Joe's Grandad was seriously ill but his mum thought he was coping well.
Joe's teacher then told mum that he was bullying other children at school.
Joe was worried about discussing his feelings at home for fear of upsetting the family. He was angry and upset. He was unable to share his feelings so he was showing them in other ways.
Joe's family started to explain things to him and to include him in caring for Grandad.
The bullying stopped.

* Acting out feelings
* Regressing to a more immature phase of development
* Sleep disturbances
* Abdominal pain
* Strong emotions such as fear, guilt, anger, sadness, envy

Children do not need to be protected from their strong emotions

If we are not honest with children about serious illness they:

* will 'pick up' that something is wrong
* may find out the truth from someone else
* can feel isolated if things are not explained to them
* may fantasise if they are not told and this can be worse than the actual reality

What is Cancer?

1. Our bodies are made up of millions of tiny cells.

2. Sometimes one of these cells keeps on making more cells when it should have stopped

3. These extra cells grow into a lump, which is called a tumour. Some tumours may be called cancer.

4. Some of the cancer cells may break off the tumour. They travel in the blood to other parts of the body where they might grow into new tumours.

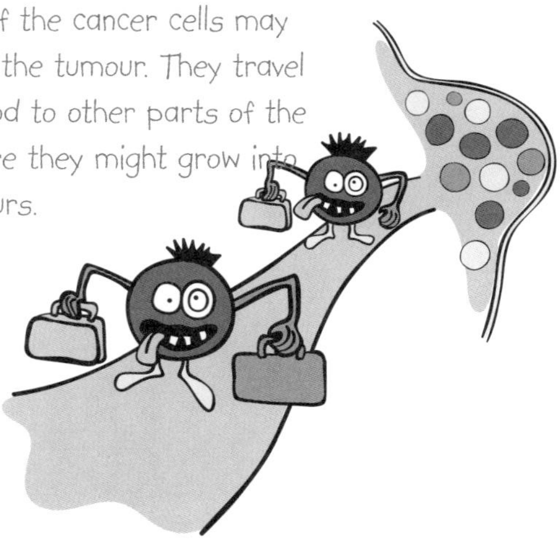

How can cancer be treated?

5. Cancer can sometimes be controlled with treatments. These treatments are called Chemotherapy and Radiotherapy. These attack the bad out-of-control cells that make the tumour.

6. Or a doctor might cut out the tumour in an operation. We hope that the bad cells will stop making more cells and the cancer will be treated.

You can't 'catch' cancer from someone who has cancer

How a Profesional Can Help

Before communicating with the child, the parents should be asked what the child has been told and whether or not they are happy for the child to be told the truth.

Ideas that may help a family:

* Provide the parents with information about the illness.
* Be honest with the children as early as possible
* Discuss with parents how they can support their children
* Suggest strategies and resources that may help parents talk to their children e.g. memory boxes, books and videos
* Include children in caring for the ill person
* Praise children for being helpful and remind parents to do so too
* Encourage children to express their feelings
* Reassure children that they are not to blame for the illness
* Give parents information on how children may grieve
* Be prepared to give on-going support to children and their parents

"only indeed, when he is given true information, and the sympathy and support to bear it, can a child or adolescent be expected to respond to his loss with any degree of realism".

(Bowlby 1980)

Breaking Bad News
To Children

Bad news is best given as soon as possible by someone who knows the child well with support of family, friends or professionals.

1. GET READY

* Know the facts because children will ask
* Find a quiet place without too many interruptions
* Choose a time when the adults are going to be around for a while - e.g. at a weekend
* Have someone around who can support you

2. ASK QUESTIONS TO FIND OUT WHAT THE CHILDREN KNOW

3. GIVE A WARNING SHOT – "I have some sad news to tell you."

4. EXPLAIN IN STEPS

5. ANSWER CHILDREN'S QUESTIONS AT THEIR OWN PACE

6. BREAK THE BAD NEWS

7. ALLOW CHILDREN TO EXPRESS FEELINGS

8. ALLOW TIME FOR QUESTIONS AND ANSWER THEM HONESTLY

9. GIVE THE INFORMATION REPEATEDLY OVER A PERIOD OF TIME

Telling a Child Someone Has Died by Suicide

There are often complex circumstances surrounding a suicide. It is helpful to take a much more thorough history to include feelings about relationships before the suicide and attitudes now to those events.

Taking the time to do this is usually very therapeutic for the adults. Afterwards the adults are usually empowered and less afraid to talk to their children openly.

* When someone has died through suicide the process of breaking bad news is the same as for any death. (See Pg 11)
* It is just as important in these circumstances to be honest with the children and tell them that their special person has died. Followed by **how** they died. This can be done in stages and does not have to happen all in one go.
* If children are not told that someone has died through suicide they may hear from others or from the news media. Thus everyone else may be discussing it but the children are unable to share their feelings or understanding at home.
* Children cope better when they know the truth even though it is often difficult to tell them.

"A child can live through anything so long as he or she is told the truth and is allowed to share the natural feelings people have when they are suffering"

(Eda Le Shan 1987)

Suicide Resource

Winston's Wish provides a helpful booklet "Beyond the Rough Rocks" which can assist adults when telling children how the person died.
ISBN: 0-09539123-3-7 Tel: 01242 515157

* Health professionals can offer support and be around at the time that the news is broken or be available to follow up and answer questions later if necessary.
* Health professionals need to take care of themselves at these times and may need to talk about their feelings concerning the situation.

How Bereaved Children Present

The majority of children with a bereavement problem will present with various misleading symptoms. Very few have bereavement as the presenting complaint; those that do represent only the tip of the iceberg.

The presentation may be

* physical
* emotional
* developmental
* behavioural
* psychological

One or a combination of signs and symptoms may be present

The presentation tends to differ according to age

How to Make the Diagnosis

* Accidents and illnesses are much more common in children who are bereaved.
* To diagnose the underlying problem you need a high index of suspicion.
* Always ask about bereavement and watch the child's reaction:
    - do they look away?
    - do the eyes moisten?
    - do they start to fidget or become unusually still?

If you don't ask about bereavement, you'll miss it

Child Bereavement-Presentation Iceberg

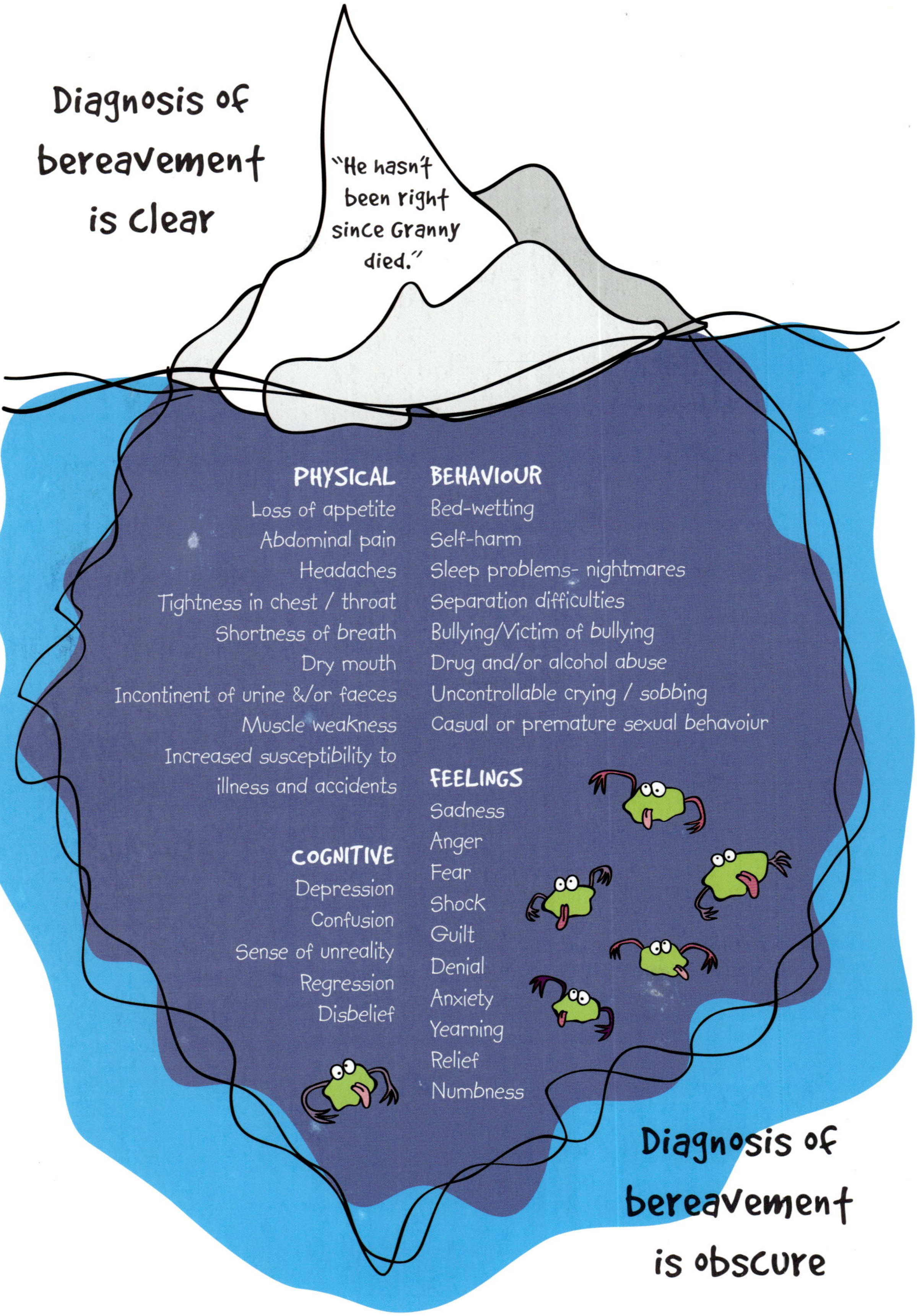

What the Health Professionals Should Do

Having recognised that bereavement is the root of the problem it is important to explain this to the parents. This alone can open communications allowing the child to talk about how they feel and enabling the parent to support the child.

Talk to the Child

This will express your understanding and care. Use language appropriate to their cognitive age and development. Reassure them that they will feel better in time. Set an example for the parents to follow.

Listen to the Child

It is rare for a child to ask questions of a doctor or other health professional – adults usually ask on their behalf. Be open with the child, not just the adults and encourage questions.

Encourage the Child to Express Themselves

Help the parents realise the importance of listening and being supportive rather than being critical or dismissive. Children can be helped to express themselves and their feelings in a variety of ways e.g. drawing or painting.

Encourage the Parents

Remembering the good times spent with the person who died will help the child. For example they could get out old photographs and mementoes.

Notify others

It may be appropriate to notify other professionals such as the GP, Health Visitor, and the School as to how the child is reacting to the bereavement. Use the form at the back of the book (see Pg 29).

Arrange Follow-Up

By now, you are involved and know a lot about this problem, and the parents and child have begun to trust you. Follow-up with you will usually be most appropriate. If this is not possible, ensure an appointment is arranged with someone else whom the child and parents trust.

Safety Netting

Ensure the child and parents understand what to do if things get worse before the next visit.

* Tell them who they should contact and how.
* They should look out for signs of complex grief (see 'When to Refer On')
* Reassure them that this is an important problem and they should call if concerned.

What other Help is Available?

In most cases the actions previously listed above can produce dramatic improvements in the presenting problem and the child's mental health, given time and support.

Child Bereavement Services

These offer support and advice to parents, children and professionals.
Some, such as Penhaligon's Friends in Cornwall, also offer:

* Activities with groups of bereaved children to aid the grieving process
* Activities for parents and carers to enable them to support their child better through the bereavement
* Advice sheets
* Books and videos
* A website
* A home visiting service
* Social activities for bereaved families
* Training for professionals and volunteers

Services for Children, Young People & their Families

These statutory services can offer specialised help for children with persistent or complex grief. A child psychologist is only needed for the most refractory of problems. Certainly, this should be considered before drug therapy or a child psychiatrist.
Social workers may get involved where bereavement is complicated by other social or behaviour problems, by family breakdown or child protection concerns.

Religious Groups

Religious groups have a role to play, especially if the family already belongs. All have views on what happens after death. They are very experienced in dealing with death since they usually become involved in the funeral service. Pastoral care is the norm with some workers having been trained specifically in child bereavement.

Holidays for Bereaved Families

Some charities are now offering free or reduced cost holidays for families who have been bereaved. This gives them a chance to have time together away from the usual pressures, to laugh and to heal. For example: The Sand Rose Project (0845 607 6357) has a holiday cottage in Cornwall.

Health Promotion Department

The local health promotion department may have resources available on child bereavement.

Websites

* www.childbereavement.org.uk (the Child Bereavement Trust)
* www.penhaligonsfriends.org.uk
* www.ncb.org.uk/cbn (Child Bereavement Network)

When to Refer on

Children exhibit signs of loss and grief in many ways, but feelings of sadness and loss usually lessen over time. It is a combination of prolonged changes in behaviour, intensity of feelings and actions that signal onward referral may be needed.

Red Flags to Identify Children Who Need on-ward Referral

* Persistent difficulty talking about the dead parent
* Persistent un-containable aggression
* Persistent symptoms of anxiety, shown by a refusal to go to school and extreme clinging to the surviving parent
* Persistent somatic complaints
* Persistent sleep difficulties

  &/or nightmares after a year
* Persistent changes in eating patterns
* Marked long-term social withdrawal
* School difficulties or a serious decline in academic performance, continuing after nine months
* Persistent self-blame or guilt (indicative of clinical depression)
* Self-destructive behaviour or desire to die: in this case, a child should be offered individual work immediately, regardless of how long ago the death occurred.

Worden W (1996) pg 147-150 as quoted in 'Then Now & Always' Stokes J

Post Traumatic Stress Reactions

Children who are bereaved may experience post traumatic stress reactions; these are more common following a traumatic death.

CHILDREN MAY:

*** Re-experience the Trauma:**

Children may have repetitive, intrusive thoughts or flashbacks about the incident. These are often triggered by something in the environment that reminds them of the incident. They tend to occur most often when the children are otherwise quiet.

*** Avoid Thinking About the Experience:**

Children may not talk to parents, siblings or peers to avoid the painful feelings and emotions or because they are worried about upsetting others.

*** Have Foreshortened Future and Change of Priorities:**

Learning how easily life can be extinguished can cause young people to lose their faith in the future. They may feel that their whole view of the world and their own priorities have been altered. Many feel that they should live each day to the full and not plan ahead. Others realise they have been over-concerned with materialistic or petty matters.

*** Experience Guilt:**

'Survivor guilt' has long been considered a paradoxical reaction following a disaster. Child and adolescent survivors often feel guilty that they are alive when others have died. They may feel guilty that they could have done more to help others during the disaster or crisis.

*** Have Heightened Anxiety and Arousal:**

This may appear as concentration difficulties, sleep disturbances, separation difficulties, memory problems, and heightened alertness to dangers, fears, irritability, depression, anxiety and panic.

If these reactions cause concern to the child or family it may be necessary to refer for further help.

Traumatic Bereavement

Following: Accidents, Suicide, Sudden Infant Death, Murder.

It is common for a child to need to talk about the traumatic event before they can deal with the bereavement itself, particularly if they have been involved in the event. Although the family may want to protect the child from the facts, this is a situation where rumours may be very unhelpful.

Common Reactions to Traumatic Grief

FEELINGS

* Intense shock, with recurring images of the death even if not witnessed.
* Sense of rejection or abandonment following suicide.
* Irritable - easily aroused by threat or upheaval, expressing extreme, unfocused rage.
* Feeling guilty for surviving
* Anxious and pre-occupied by the trauma, specifically about threats of similar danger.
* Withdrawal and avoidance of feelings

RELATIONSHIPS

* Strained family relationships- often resulting in blame
* Stigma and isolation from the community.

RESPONSES

* Avoiding objects, places and events that are associated with the event.
* Heightened awareness to threat and danger.
* Difficulties retaining pleasant memories- replaced by intrusive pictures or fantasies of the event.
* Prolonged search for a reason or explanation of the tragedy.
* Problems with sleeping including nightmares.

This group of children is more at risk of prolonged or unresolved grief. They should all be offered follow-up appointments to monitor progress.

Section E

The Death of a Baby or Child

How Professionals Can Help

How professionals communicate with and support parents at the time of a death can profoundly affect their experience of the loss of their child, and may influence how they support their other children.

As there are often traumatic circumstances surrounding the death of a baby or child, it is important to give the parents and children time to talk about their worries and anxieties.

Parents and children need:

* To be encouraged to spend time with the baby both before and after the death, in private and appropriate surroundings.
* Parents need to be reassured that inviting the child to be involved in such things as viewing the body, planning the funeral and other activities can often be helpful at the time and will assist with the grieving process in the future.
* Signposting to other organisations will enable them to meet with other parents who have experienced the death of a baby. See list of supportive organisations inside back cover.

There are several reasons why children may have difficulties grieving:

* They may have little or no memories of their dead sibling therefore it is difficult for them to accept the reality of the loss
* Their sibling may have had a long and complicated illness, and they may have been separated for some time.
* Children may have found their sibling dead and witnessed the resuscitation.

To help them grieve children need:

* **INFORMATION**
  About the illness and death of the baby as soon as possible. This should be spoken in words that the child understands.
* **To BE INCLUDED**
  Children who have been included and see their dead baby have a better understanding of what has happened and experience less fear and bewilderment.
* **To BE REASSURED**
  Children need to know that the baby's death is nothing to do with their thoughts or actions and that they are not to blame.
* **EXTRA STABILITY**
  Children find this period of time very confusing and a return to routine will help them to feel more secure.
* **To EXPRESS FEELINGS**
  Children need to know their parents love them and that life will not always be so sad. Parents should encourage their children to talk and express their feelings by sharing their own sadness at this time. Hugs can be very healing.

Children with Special Needs

Children with Special Needs are just as likely to experience bereavement. They often need to be monitored even more closely, as they are more likely to require ongoing support.

Children can have a wide range of special needs:

* Visual and hearing impairment
* Speech and language difficulties
* Communication disorders
* Various physical and/or learning difficulties
* Behavioural, emotional and social difficulties

Some children have special needs, which are profound and complex.

Helpful Interventions

* Things should be kept as clear and simple as possible
* To be given information appropriate for their developmental stage and understanding, rather than chronological age.
* Information may need to be repeated again and again.
* A variety of methods can be used to help them express their grief e.g. art and play.
* Involve the professional who has the specialist experience of working with children in this area e.g. teacher of the deaf.

In general, the grief responses will be similar to those expressed by other children. However, they may be more pronounced and prolonged if the child is having difficulty understanding what is going on around them and letting others know how they feel.

With the right kind of intervention, these children can be helped to explore and come to terms with their feelings about the events that have taken place, and can be supported by professionals through this process.

Spiritual & cultural Issues

"Health is a state of complete physical, mental, social and spiritual well-being and not merely the absence of disease or infirmity"
(The World Health organisation - constitution)

It is important to consider the family's spiritual values, beliefs, race and cultural heritage as this may have an effect on the grieving process and the child's behaviour.

> "No-one can ever be categorised solely in terms of their cultural and religious background, but there has been a heightened interest in how these factors may, sensitively understood, much enhance the quality of care. Mistakes, miscommunications, and misconceptions can be avoided if religious beliefs and practices are properly understood by those who come into contact with the dying and bereaved"
> (Ian Ainsworth Smith)

SPIRITUAL ISSUES

This area is often difficult for health professionals but it should not be neglected. A bereaved child may never before have considered life's huge questions such as: "Where's heaven?"
When considering spiritual belief the following tips may by helpful:

* Firstly find out about the family's belief system
* Listen to the child's concerns about spiritual issues even if you don't know the answers
* Respect the spiritual beliefs
* Be careful not to impose personal belief systems on the bereaved child
* Involve the parents and help them find an appropriate source of spiritual support e.g. Priest, Rabbi, Imam, Counsellor.

"Supporting a child as they explore spiritual issues can be an intrinsic part of the grieving process."

CULTURAL ISSUES

The following tips may be especially helpful:

* In order to be able to identify "unusual" or problem behaviour it may be helpful to find out about a child's "usual" behaviour and cultural/ethnic responses.
* It is important to realise that talking openly is not comfortable, appropriate, or even "polite" in some cultures.
* In some cultures making eye contact is not accepted. For some groups it is considered to be "defiant behaviour", whereas lack of eye contact in other cultures is seen as an indication that the person is being less than truthful.
* Keep in mind when helping children to express themselves through art activities, that colours and shapes have various meanings to children from different cultures, and to different children within each culture.
* Children who have experienced loss resulting from relocation, war or terrorism may be at higher risk of serious bereavement problems.
* These children are more likely than others to have flashbacks, e.g. loud noises associated with memories of bombings.

Looking After Yourself

When working alongside children there will always be a strong desire to make things better. However, it is not about taking the pain away, but working through the emotions and helping the young person to adapt.

It is emotionally demanding for anybody supporting a grieving child and this can create stress on professionals in the following ways:

* Previous personal losses may resurface when dealing with the bereavement of others.
* Some professionals may not be comfortable with the level of emotion.
* Dealing with a bereaved family can be very stressful due to the various needs of the individuals.
* If emotional demands come on top of other difficulties this can add to stress and create extra workload.
* Professionals who are already dealing with personal or work difficulties will find bereavement work especially draining.
* The professional lacks confidence.

What Helps:

* Health-care professionals dealing with a death need to be aware of the support available to them. This may include supervision, counselling, supportive colleagues and occupational health services.
* Reassurance about helping the family can be gained from experienced colleagues or childhood bereavement groups e.g. Penhaligon's Friends.
* Sharing the load by involving others in caring for the child and family.
* Referring on.
* Training in 'Childhood Grief'.

Section F

Bereaved Child Notification

This form is to notify you that one or more of the children you have contact with have been bereaved

Names of bereaved children		Date of birth
1		
2		
3		

Person who has died (name & relationship to child)

Date of Death		Cause of Death	
Other professional supporting family			

Further information

(Please continue overleaf)

Parents or guardians details

Name	
Relationship to Child	
Address	
Telephone	

Notification sent by

I agree to this information being shared with other professionals:

Signature: .... (Parent/Guardian) Date: ....

Recommended Reading

Books for Children & Teenagers

Finding a Way Through When Someone Close Has Died - Mood P & Whittaker L
ISBN: 1853029203
A workbook written and illustrated by young people for children. It gives advice, based on their own experiences on how to cope with the practical and emotional upheavals of bereavement.

Goodbye Grandma - Brauna D
ISBN: 1405219017
Miffy the children's favorite character is sad when her grandma died. Suitable for children 3-5yrs

Help For The Hard Times - Hipp E
ISBN: 1-56838-085-5
This book looks at different kinds of loss, grief & skills to help teenagers

How it feels When a Parent Dies - Kremetz J
ISBN 0 394 75854 4

I Miss You - Thomas P
ISBN: 0764117645
A First Look at Death

Missing Mum - Mitchell L
ISBN: 1900339021
Story about Lucy and her worries about who will look after her when her mum is in hospital.

The Secret C - Stokes J
ISBN: 0953912302
Straight Talking About Cancer

Waterbugs and Dragonflies - Stickney D
ISBN: 0-826-46458-0
Pocket book to help explain death to children

What on Earth Do You Do When Someone Dies? - Romain T
ISBN: 1575420554
A book that gives answers to many of the questions children have after someone close dies.

When Dinosaurs Die - Brown LK, Brown M
ISBN: 0316119555
This factual picture book covers many issues including 'why does someone die?', 'feelings about death' and 'saying goodbye'. An excellent resource for anyone caring for young children.

Recommended Reading

Books & Workbooks for Parents & Professionals

As Big as it Gets - Winstons Wish ISBN: 0-9539123-2-9
Supporting a child when someone is seriously ill.

Beyond the Rough Rock - Winstons Wish ISBN 0-953912333-3-7
Supporting a child bereaved through suicide.

Coping with Loss - Elliot P ISBN 1 85340 453 5

Forgotten Mourners - Smith Sc ISBN: 1853027588
Guidelines for working with bereaved children.

Grief Encounter - Gilbert S ISBN: 1-904787-21-5
A workbook to encourage conversations about loss between children and adults.

Grief in Children - Dyregov A ISBN: 1-85302-113-X

I Saw It Happen - Deaton W ISBN:0-89793-241-2
A workbook for adults working with children who have witnessed events involving violence, such as kidnappings, murders, fires and traumatic accidents.

Muddles, Puddles and Sunshine - Winston's Wish ISBN: 1-86989058-2
A book of activities and exercises to offer an outlet for difficult feelings to be expressed and for children to reflect on their grief experience.

Supporting Sick Children and their Families - Cook P ISBN: 0-7020-2207-1

Then Now & Always - Stokes J A ISBN 0-9539123-5-3
Manual of interventions for community based children's bereavement service.

The Grieving Child - Fitzgerald H ISBN: 0133632261
Excellent help for parents supporting grieving children.

When a Parent has Cancer - Harpham W S ISBN:0-06-074081-7

When Someone has a Very Serious Illness- Heegard M ISBN: 0-9620502-4-5

When Someone Very Special Has Died - Heegard M ISBN;0-9620502-0-2

For Your Appraisal / Personal Development Folder

Now you have read this book, please photocopy and complete this form. Fax it to us, so we can improve the next edition, and drop it into your appraisal folder / personal development folder as a record of this educational activity and your reflection on what you have learned.

Book Review

Remember Me Too. Child Bereavement in a Nutshell.
A Handbook for Busy Health Care Professionals.
Published by Penhaligon's Friends, 2006. ISBN 0-9550757-1-8

I finished reading this book on:

What I thought of the book:

What I learned from it:

This is how it will affect my practice:

My opinion of this book. Please circle as appropriate. 0=useless, 10=cannot be improved!

Content	0	1	2	3	4	5	6	7	8	9	10
Style	0	1	2	3	4	5	6	7	8	9	10
Relevance to me	0	1	2	3	4	5	6	7	8	9	10

I think the next edition could be improved by:

Name
Job role

Now please send this form to Penhaligon's Friends, Fax: 07050 699526. Thank you.

References & Bibliography

Ainsworth-Smith I (2005) Ethical Issues in Palliative Care - Second Edition Radcliffe Publishing

Dyregrov A (1992) Grief in Children - Jessica Kingsley Publishers

Worden W (1996) Children and Grief - The Guildford Press, New York

Wordon W (1991) Grief Counselling and Grief Therapy - Brunner/ Routledge New York

Wasss H, Corr CA (1984) Childhood and Death - Hemisphere Publishing Corporation, Washington DC

Grollman EA (1990) Talking about Death - Beacon Press, Boston

Notes